Greatest Ever

Thai

The All Time Top 20 Greatest Recipes

Greatest Ever

Thai

The All Time Top 20 Greatest Recipes

p

This is a Parragon Book
First published in 2002

Parragon
Queen Street House
4 Queen Street
Bath BA1 1HE, UK

ISBN: 0-75256-852-3

Printed in China

NOTE

This book uses metric and imperial measurements. Follow the same
units of measurement throughout; do not mix metric and imperial.
All spoon measurements are level: teaspoons are assumed to be 5 ml,
and tablespoons are assumed to be 15 ml. Unless otherwise stated,
milk is assumed to be full fat, eggs and individual vegetables such as
potatoes are medium, and pepper is freshly ground black pepper.

The times given for each recipe are an approximate guide only
because the preparation times may differ according to the techniques
used by different people and the cooking times may vary as a result
of the type of oven used. The preparation times include marinating,
chilling and freezing times, where appropriate.

Recipes using raw or very lightly cooked eggs should be
avoided by infants, the elderly, pregnant women, convalescents,
and anyone suffering from an illness.

CONTENTS

INTRODUCTION

Thai food uses a distinctive, unique blend of fragrant, piquant and spicy flavours, such as lemon grass, limes and chillies. Thai cooks create wonderfully colourful and refreshing dishes, most often based around fish and seafood – meat is usually reserved for special celebrations. Chicken is much more common than beef and it is not unusual to see chicken (or pork) combined with seafood such as shrimp or crab meat. Duck is a Thai favourite, however, barbecued in warm spices, soy sauce or sweet glazes.

The structure of a Thai meal is more flexible than in the West, with no starter or main course as such; instead soups, side dishes, noodles, rice and main dishes are served simultaneously.

Rice is a staple food in Thailand and hardly a meal goes by without it appearing in some form or another. Two main varieties are used – a fluffy long grain fragrant rice, and a stickier round grain. Noodles also play a vital part in Thai cookery. Rice noodles in flat ribbons or thin vermicelli are the types most commonly used. They need to be soaked before they are stir-fried or added to soups.

A Thai meal usually ends with a basket of delicious fresh tropical fruits, such as mangoes and lychees.

Above: Easy-to-make Thai morsels such as deep-fried fritters or fish cakes are ideal as a starter for an Oriental feast.

various chillies

The essential ingredients when you start cooking Thai dishes are coconut, lime, chilli, garlic, lemon grass, ginger, coriander and rice. Armed with these, you can recreate many typical Thai dishes with an authentic flavour and texture in your own kitchen.

Thai principles

The main principle of Thai cookery is to balance the five extremes of flavour – bitter, sour, hot, salty and sweet – in a single dish, or across a selection of dishes. Each part of a Thai meal is chosen to contribute to the perfect balance of the whole feast.

Don't be daunted by the long list of ingredients in some of the recipes. The methods are easy for even an inexperienced cook to master quickly.

Right: Many Thai meals are based around seafood and lightly-cooked vegetables, and can be healthy and low in fat.

Hot stuff

Chilli plays a prominent role in Thai curries, which are traditionally very hot and designed to make a little go a long way. Thin, highly spiced juices are eaten with lots of rice to stretch a small amount of meat as far as possible. As you become more familiar with each recipe you will develop a sixth sense of how to adjust the spiciness to suit your own taste.

red pepper

baby corn cobs

mussels

lobster

basil

coriander

chillies

Most of the basic Thai flavourings are now widely available from general supermarkets as well as specialist Asian food shops.

THE THAI STORE-CUPBOARD

coconut

dried chilli seeds

lemon grass

noodles

Basil

Three types of sweet basil are used in Thai cooking, but the sweet basil familiar from Italian cooking also works well. Asian food shops often sell seeds for growing Thai basil at home.

Chillies

The many varieties of chilli vary in heat, from very mild to fiery hot, so choose carefully. The small red or green 'bird-eye' chillies often used in Thai dishes are very hot. If you prefer a milder spiciness, remove the seeds. Red chillies are usually slightly sweeter and milder than green. Large chillies tend to be milder than small ones. Dried crushed chillies are used for seasoning.

Coconut milk

This is not the liquid found inside coconuts (which is called coconut water) – it is made from grating and pressing fresh white coconut flesh. You can buy it in cans, in powdered form or in blocks as creamed coconut. Coconut cream is skimmed from the top of the milk and is slightly thicker and richer.

Coriander

With its light, citrus-like flavour, this herb is widely used in savoury Thai dishes.

Fish sauce

Called *nam pla*, Thai fish sauce has a distinctive, intense aroma. It is a salty brown liquid made from fermented fish, and is widely used as a seasoning.

Galangal

This relative of ginger with a milder aromatic flavour is available fresh or dried.

garlic

brown sugar

Garlic

Garlic is used extensively in Thai cuisine, whole, crushed, sliced or chopped.

Ginger

Fresh root ginger is popular in Thai dishes for its warm, spicy flavour and aroma. It will keep for several weeks in a cool, dry place.

Kaffir lime leaves

Glossy, dark green kaffir lime leaves have a distinctive citrus flavour. They can be bought fresh, dried or frozen. If you have difficulty finding them, the grated zest of a fresh lime can be used as an alternative.

Lemon grass

This aromatic tropical grass has a lemon scent similar to the herb lemon balm. Strip off the fibrous outer leaves and slice or finely chop the rest, or bruise and use whole.

Palm sugar

This is a rich, brown, unrefined sugar from the coconut palm, sold in solid blocks which need crushing. Dark brown sugar is an acceptable substitute.

Rice vinegar

Also called mirin, golden rice vinegar is used in Thai dishes as a savoury flavouring. Sherry or wine vinegar can be used as alternatives.

Soy sauce

Both dark and light soy sauce can be used to season dishes. Light soy sauce is saltier than the dark version.

Tamarind

The pulp of the tamarind pod is usually sold in blocks, and is used to give a sweet/sour flavour. Soak the pulp in hot water for 30 minutes, press out the juice and discard the pulp and seeds.

limes and lime leaves

root ginger

fragrant coconut rice

spatula

wooden spoon

EQUIPMENT

Steamer

A steamer can be used for the gentle cooking required in recipes such as Steamed Yellow Fish Fillets. It is a perforated container which sits on top of a saucepan and allows the food to be cooked in the steam generated by boiling water underneath.

You can buy a steamer to match your saucepans, or you can buy a 'universal' steamer – a perforated pan with its own lid, which will fit on top of a variety of saucepan sizes.

If you don't have a steamer, you can improvise by placing the food in a large metal colander over a pan of boiling water and covering the top with an upturned plate to trap the steam.

While cooking, always keep an eye on the water in the base of a steamer to make sure it does not boil dry. Refill it with extra boiling water from a kettle if necessary.

Wok

A wok is a deep, rounded pan which is often used for Thai stir-fries and stews. It works best on a gas cooker, but can be supported on a collar for use over an electric ring on its hottest setting. If you don't have a wok, a large frying pan can be used instead.

Kitchen foil

Foil can be used to wrap whole fish in parcels with seasoning, ready for baking. This seals in the flavour.

Pestle and mortar

A pestle and mortar is useful for grinding fresh herbs and spices to make flavoured pastes, such as Thai red curry paste. Pastes are often used as a basis for Thai marinades and cooking sauces.

vegetable knife

cooks knife

Knives

Thais take pride in presenting food beautifully, often carving vegetables and fruit into elaborate shapes as a garnish. It takes practice and a sharp, small vegetable knife to emulate such skills. As a start, you can craft delicate chilli shapes by carefully slicing a thin red chilli into strips from just under the top to the tip (leave the strips attached at the top). Then drop the whole chilli into a bowl of iced water and watch the strips curl back into a bright red 'flower', making an attractive and impressive garnish for a spicy dish.

Right and left: Thai cookery can be creative using only the most basic kitchen equipment.

grater

food processor

Food processor

A food processor can save a great deal of preparation time, chopping stir-fry ingredients to a required thickness at the touch of a button, or blending herb and spice pastes in seconds.

Wooden spatula

Use one or two strong wooden spatulas for stirring and turning over stir-fried food in a wok.

steamer

COCONUT & CRAB SOUP

>Serves 4   >Preparation time: 5 minutes   >Cooking time: 10 minutes

INGREDIENTS

1 tbsp groundnut oil

2 tbsp Thai red curry paste

1 red pepper, deseeded and sliced

600 ml/1 pint coconut milk

600 ml/1 pint fish stock

2 tbsp Thai fish sauce

225 g/8 oz canned or fresh white crab meat

225 g/8 oz fresh or frozen crab claws

2 tbsp chopped fresh coriander

3 spring onions, topped and tailed and sliced

METHOD

1 Heat the oil in a preheated wok or large frying pan.

2 Add the red curry paste and red pepper to the wok and stir-fry for 1 minute.

3 Add the coconut milk, fish stock and fish sauce and bring to the boil.

4 Add the crab meat, crab claws, coriander and spring onions to the wok.

5 Stir the mixture well and heat thoroughly for 2–3 minutes or until warmed through.

6 Transfer the soup into warmed bowls and serve hot.

THAI FISH SOUP

>Serves 4　>Preparation time: 10 minutes　>Cooking time: 25 minutes

INGREDIENTS

450 ml/16 fl oz light chicken stock

2 lime leaves, chopped

5-cm/2-inch piece of lemon grass, chopped

3 tbsp lemon juice

3 tbsp Thai fish sauce

2 small, hot green chillies, deseeded and finely chopped

½ tsp sugar

8 small shiitake mushrooms or 8 straw mushrooms, halved

450 g/1 lb raw prawns, peeled and deveined

sliced spring onions, to garnish

TOM YAM SAUCE

4 tbsp vegetable oil

5 garlic cloves, finely chopped

1 large shallot, finely chopped

2 large hot dried red chillies, roughly chopped

1 tbsp dried shrimp, optional

1 tbsp Thai fish sauce

2 tsp sugar

METHOD

1 First make the tom yam sauce. Heat the oil in a small frying pan and add the garlic. Cook for a few seconds until the garlic just browns. Remove with a slotted spoon and set aside. Add the shallot to the same oil and fry until browned and crisp. Remove with a slotted spoon and set aside. Add the chillies and fry until they darken. Remove from the oil and drain on kitchen paper. Remove the frying pan from the hob and set aside with the oil.

2 In a small food processor or spice grinder, grind the dried shrimp, if using, then add the reserved chillies, garlic and shallots. Grind together to a smooth paste. Return the pan with the original oil to a low heat, add the paste and warm. Add the fish sauce and sugar and mix. Remove from the heat.

3 In a large saucepan, heat together the stock and 2 tablespoons of the tom yam sauce. Add the lime leaves, lemon grass, lemon juice, fish sauce, chillies and sugar. Simmer for 2 minutes.

4 Add the mushrooms and prawns and continue simmering for 2–3 minutes until the prawns are cooked. Ladle into warmed bowls and serve hot, garnished with spring onions.

VEGETABLE SPRING ROLLS

>Serves 4   >Preparation time: 10 minutes   >Cooking time: 15 minutes

INGREDIENTS

225 g/8 oz carrots

1 red pepper

2 tbsp sunflower oil

75 g/2¾ oz beansprouts

finely grated zest and juice of 1 lime

1 red chilli, deseeded and finely chopped

1 tbsp soy sauce

½ tsp arrowroot

2 tbsp chopped fresh coriander

8 sheets filo pastry

2 tbsp butter

2 tsp sesame oil

TO SERVE

chilli sauce

spring onion tassels

METHOD

1 Using a sharp knife, cut the carrots into thin sticks. Deseed the pepper and slice thinly.

2 Heat 1 tablespoon of the sunflower oil in a preheated wok or large frying pan.

3 Add the carrot, pepper and beansprouts and cook, stirring, for 2 minutes, or until softened. Remove the wok from the heat and toss in the lime zest and juice, and the red chilli.

4 Mix the soy sauce with the arrowroot and stir into the mixture in the wok. Return the wok to the heat and cook for 2 minutes or until the juices have thickened.

5 Add the chopped fresh coriander to the wok and mix well.

6 Lay the sheets of filo pastry out on a board. Melt the butter and sesame oil and brush each sheet with the mixture.

7 Spoon a little of the vegetable filling on to the top of each sheet, fold over each long side, and roll up.

8 Add the remaining oil to the wok and cook the spring rolls, in batches, for 2–3 minutes or until crisp and golden.

9 Transfer the spring rolls to a serving dish, garnish and serve hot with chilli dipping sauce.

THAI NOODLES

>Serves 4 >Preparation time: 5 minutes >Cooking time: 10–15 minutes

INGREDIENTS

350 g/12 oz cooked, peeled tiger prawns

115 g/4 oz flat rice noodles or rice vermicelli

4 tbsp vegetable oil

2 garlic cloves, finely chopped

1 egg

2 tbsp lemon juice

1½ tbsp Thai fish sauce

½ tsp sugar

2 tbsp chopped roasted peanuts

½ tsp cayenne pepper

2 spring onions, cut into 2.5-cm/1-inch pieces

50 g/1¾ oz fresh beansprouts

1 tbsp chopped fresh coriander

lemon wedges, to serve

METHOD

1 Drain the prawns on kitchen paper to remove excess moisture. Cook the rice noodles or vermicelli. Drain well and set aside.

2 Heat the oil in a frying pan. Fry the garlic until golden. Add the egg and stir to break it up. Cook for a few seconds.

3 Add the prawns and noodles and mix thoroughly with the egg and garlic.

4 Add the lemon juice, fish sauce, sugar, half of the peanuts, the cayenne pepper, spring onions and half of the beansprouts, stirring quickly all the time. Cook the mixture over a high heat for a further 2 minutes.

5 Turn on to a serving plate. Top with the remaining peanuts and beansprouts and sprinkle with chopped coriander. Serve with lemon wedges.

SPICY SWEETCORN FRITTERS

>Serves 4 >Preparation time: 5 minutes >Cooking time: 15 minutes

INGREDIENTS

225 g/8 oz canned or frozen sweetcorn kernels

2 red chillies, deseeded and finely chopped

2 cloves garlic, crushed

10 lime leaves, finely chopped

2 tbsp chopped fresh coriander

1 large egg

75 g/2¼ oz polenta

100 g/3½ oz fine green beans, finely sliced

groundnut oil, for frying

METHOD

1 Place the sweetcorn, chillies, garlic, lime leaves, coriander, egg and polenta in a large mixing bowl, and stir to combine.

2 Add the green beans to the ingredients in the bowl and mix well, using a wooden spoon.

3 Divide the mixture into small, evenly-sized balls. Flatten the balls of mixture between the palms of your hands to form rounds.

4 Heat a little groundnut oil in a preheated wok or large frying pan until really hot. Cook the fritters, in batches, until brown and crispy on the outside, turning occasionally.

5 Leave the fritters to drain on kitchen paper while frying the remainder.

6 Transfer the drained fritters to warmed serving plates and serve hot.

RED-HOT BEEF WITH CASHEWS

> Serves 4   > Preparation time: 2 hours 15 minutes   > Cooking time: 8 minutes

INGREDIENTS

500 g/1 lb 2 oz boneless, lean beef sirloin, thinly sliced

1 tsp vegetable oil

MARINADE

1 tbsp sesame seeds

1 garlic clove, chopped

1 tbsp fresh root ginger, finely chopped

1 red bird-eye chilli, chopped

2 tbsp dark soy sauce

1 tsp red curry paste

TO FINISH

1 tsp sesame oil

4 tbsp unsalted cashew nuts

1 spring onion, thickly sliced diagonally

cucumber slices, to garnish

METHOD

1 Cut the beef into 1 cm/½ inch wide strips. Place them in a large, non-metallic bowl.

2 To make the marinade, toast the sesame seeds in a heavy-based pan over a medium heat for 2–3 minutes until golden brown, shaking the pan occasionally.

3 Place the seeds in a pestle and mortar with the garlic, ginger and chilli, and grind to a smooth paste. Add the soy sauce and curry paste and mix well.

4 Spoon the paste over the beef strips and toss well to coat the meat evenly. Cover and leave to marinate in the refrigerator for 2–3 hours, or overnight.

5 Heat a heavy frying pan or griddle until very hot and brush with vegetable oil. Add the beef strips and cook quickly, turning often, until lightly browned. Remove from the heat and spoon onto a hot serving dish.

6 Heat the sesame oil in a small pan and quickly fry the cashew nuts until golden. Take care that they do not burn. Add the spring onions and stir-fry for 30 seconds. Sprinkle the mixture on top of the beef strips and serve immediately garnished with cucumber slices.

CHILLI COCONUT CHICKEN

>Serves 4   >Preparation time: 5 minutes   >Cooking time: 15 minutes

INGREDIENTS

150 ml/5 fl oz hot chicken stock

25 g/1 oz creamed coconut

1 tbsp sunflower oil

8 skinless, boneless chicken thighs, cut into long, thin strips

1 small red chilli, thinly sliced

4 spring onions, thinly sliced

4 tbsp smooth or crunchy peanut butter

finely grated rind and juice of 1 lime

boiled rice, to serve

TO GARNISH

1 small red chilli

spring onion tassel

METHOD

1 Pour the chicken stock into a measuring jug or small bowl. Crumble the creamed coconut into the chicken stock and stir the mixture until the coconut dissolves.

2 Heat the oil in a preheated wok or large, heavy-based frying pan.

3 Add the chicken strips and cook, stirring, until the chicken turns a golden colour.

4 Stir in the chopped red chilli and spring onions and cook gently for a few minutes.

5 Add the peanut butter, coconut and chicken stock mixture, lime rind and juice and simmer, uncovered, for about 5 minutes, stirring frequently to prevent the mixture sticking to the base of the wok.

6 Transfer the chilli coconut chicken to a warmed serving dish, garnish with the red chilli and spring onion tassel and serve with boiled rice.

RED LAMB CURRY

>Serves 4 >Preparation time: 10 minutes >Cooking time: 35–40 minutes

INGREDIENTS

500 g/1 lb 2 oz boneless lean leg of lamb

2 tbsp vegetable oil

1 large onion, sliced

2 garlic cloves, crushed

2 tbsp Thai red curry paste

150 ml/5 fl oz coconut milk

1 tbsp soft light brown sugar

1 large red pepper, deseeded and thickly sliced

125 ml/4 fl oz lamb or beef stock

1 tbsp Thai fish sauce

2 tbsp lime juice

225 g/8 oz canned water chestnuts, drained

2 tbsp chopped fresh coriander

2 tbsp chopped fresh basil

salt and pepper

boiled jasmine rice, to serve

fresh basil leaves, to garnish

METHOD

1 Trim the meat and cut into 3-cm/1¼-inch cubes. Heat the oil in a frying pan over a high heat and fry the onion and crushed garlic for 2–3 minutes to soften. Add the meat and fry until lightly browned.

2 Stir in the curry paste and cook for a few seconds, then add the coconut milk and sugar and bring to the boil. Reduce the heat and simmer for 15 minutes, stirring occasionally.

3 Stir in the red pepper, stock, fish sauce and lime juice, cover and continue simmering for a further 15 minutes, or until the meat is tender.

4 Add the water chestnuts, coriander and basil. Adjust the seasoning to taste. Serve with jasmine rice garnished with fresh basil leaves.

PAK CHOI WITH CRAB MEAT

>Serves 4 >Preparation time: 5 minutes >Cooking time: 8 minutes

INGREDIENTS

2 heads green pak choi, about 250 g/9 oz
total weight

2 tbsp vegetable oil

1 garlic clove, thinly sliced

2 tbsp oyster sauce

100 g/3½ oz cherry tomatoes, halved

175 g/6 oz canned white crab meat, drained

salt and pepper

METHOD

1 Trim the pak choi and cut into 2.5-cm/1-inch thick slices.

2 Heat the oil in a wok or large, heavy-based frying pan and stir-fry the garlic quickly over a high heat for 1 minute.

3 Add the sliced pak choi to the wok and stir-fry for 2–3 minutes, until the leaves wilt but the stalks are still crisp.

4 Add the oyster sauce and tomatoes and stir-fry for a further minute.

5 Add the crab meat and season well with salt and pepper. Stir well to heat thoroughly and evenly distribute the crab before serving.

STIR-FRIED VEGETABLES

>Serves 4 >Preparation time: 35–40 minutes >Cooking time: 10 minutes

INGREDIENTS

1 aubergine

2 tbsp vegetable oil

3 garlic cloves, crushed

4 spring onions, chopped

1 small red pepper, deseeded and sliced

4 baby corn cobs, halved lengthways

85 g/3 oz mangetouts

200 g/7 oz Chinese mustard greens, roughly shredded

425 g/15 oz canned Chinese straw mushrooms, drained

125 g/4½ oz beansprouts

2 tbsp rice wine

2 tbsp yellow bean sauce

2 tbsp dark soy sauce

1 tsp chilli sauce

1 tsp sugar

125 ml/4 fl oz chicken or vegetable stock

1 tsp cornflour

2 tsp water

salt

METHOD

1 Trim the aubergine and cut into 5-cm/2-inch matchsticks. Place in a colander, sprinkle with salt and let drain for 30 minutes. Rinse in cold water and pat dry.

2 Heat the oil in a wok or large frying pan and stir-fry the garlic, spring onions and pepper over a high heat for 1 minute. Stir in the aubergine and stir-fry for a further minute, or until softened.

3 Stir in the baby corn and mangetouts and stir-fry for about 1 minute. Add the mustard greens, mushrooms and beansprouts and stir-fry for 30 seconds.

4 Mix together the rice wine, yellow bean sauce, soy sauce, chilli sauce and sugar and add to the wok with the stock. Bring to the boil, stirring.

5 Slowly blend the cornflour with the water to form a smooth paste. Stir quickly into the wok and cook for a further minute. Serve hot.

JASMINE RICE

>Serves 4   >Preparation time: 5 minutes   >Cooking time: 20–25 minutes

INGREDIENTS

400 g/14 oz jasmine rice

800 ml/1⅓ pints water

finely grated rind of ½ lemon

2 tbsp chopped fresh sweet basil

METHOD

1 Rinse the rice thoroughly under cold running water until the water runs completely clear.

2 Bring the water to the boil in a large pan, then add the rice. Bring the water back to a rolling boil. Turn the heat to a low simmer, cover the pan and cook for 12 minutes.

3 Remove the pan from the heat and leave to stand, covered, for about 10 minutes.

4 Fluff up the rice with a fork, then stir in the lemon rind. Serve scattered with basil.

FRAGRANT COCONUT RICE

>Serves 4   >Preparation time: 5 minutes   >Cooking time: 15–20 minutes

INGREDIENTS

275 g/9½ oz long-grain white rice

600 ml/1 pint water

½ tsp salt

100 ml/3½ fl oz coconut milk

25 g/1 oz desiccated coconut

coconut strips, to garnish

METHOD

1 Rinse the rice thoroughly under cold running water until the water runs completely clear.

2 Place the rice in a wok with the water. Add the salt and coconut milk to the wok and bring to the boil.

3 Cover the wok with its lid, or with a lid made of foil, curved into a domed shape and resting on the sides of the wok. Reduce the heat and leave to simmer for 10 minutes.

4 Remove the lid from the wok and fluff up the rice with a fork – all of the liquid should be absorbed and the rice grains should be tender. If not, add more water and simmer for a few more minutes until all the liquid is absorbed.

5 Spoon the rice into a warmed serving bowl, scatter with the dessicated coconut and garnish with coconut strips. Serve hot.

STEAMED YELLOW FISH FILLETS

>Serves 4   >Preparation time: 15–20 minutes   >Cooking time: 12–15 minutes

INGREDIENTS

500 g/1 lb 2 oz firm fish fillets, such as red snapper, sole or monkfish

1 dried red bird-eye chilli

1 small onion, chopped

3 garlic cloves, chopped

2 sprigs fresh coriander

1 tsp coriander seeds

½ tsp turmeric

½ tsp ground black pepper

1 tbsp Thai fish sauce

2 tbsp coconut milk

1 small egg, beaten

2 tbsp rice flour

red and green chilli strips, to garnish

TO SERVE

soy sauce

stir-fried vegetables

METHOD

1 Remove any skin from the fish fillets and cut them diagonally into long strips, about 2-cm/¾-inch wide.

2 Place the dried chilli, onion, garlic, fresh coriander and coriander seeds in a pestle and mortar and grind into a smooth paste.

3 Add the turmeric, pepper, fish sauce, coconut milk and beaten egg, stirring well to mix.

4 Dip the fish strips into the paste mixture, then into the rice flour to coat lightly.

5 Bring the water in the bottom of a steamer to the boil, then arrange the fish strips in the top of the steamer. Cover and steam for about 12–15 minutes until the fish is just firm.

6 Garnish the fish with chilli strips and serve with soy sauce and stir-fried vegetables.

CRISPY DUCK WITH NOODLES

>Serves 4 >Preparation time: 1 hour 10 minutes >Cooking time: 20 minutes

INGREDIENTS

3 duck breasts, total weight about 400 g/14 oz

2 garlic cloves, crushed

1½ tsp chilli paste

1 tbsp honey

3 tbsp dark soy sauce

½ tsp Chinese five-spice powder

250 g/9 oz rice stick noodles

1 tsp vegetable oil

1 tsp sesame oil

2 spring onions, sliced

100 g/3½ oz mangetouts

2 tbsp tamarind juice

sesame seeds, to garnish

METHOD

1 Prick the skin of the duck breasts all over with a fork and place them in a deep dish.

2 Mix together the garlic, chilli, honey, soy sauce and five-spice powder, then pour over the duck. Turn the breasts over to coat them evenly, then cover and leave to marinate in the refrigerator for at least 1 hour.

3 Meanwhile, soak the rice noodles in hot water for 15 minutes. Drain well.

4 Drain the duck breasts, reserving the marinade, and grill on a rack under high heat for about 10 minutes, turning occasionally, until golden brown. Remove the duck breasts and slice them thinly.

5 Heat the vegetable and sesame oils in a frying pan and toss the spring onions and mangetouts for 2 minutes. Stir in the reserved marinade and tamarind juice and bring the mixture to the boil.

6 Add the sliced duck and noodles to the frying pan and toss to heat thoroughly. Serve hot, sprinkled with sesame seeds.

VEGETABLES IN PEANUT SAUCE

>Serves 4 >Preparation time: 15–20 minutes >Cooking time: 10 minutes

INGREDIENTS

2 carrots, peeled

1 small head cauliflower, trimmed

2 small heads green pak choi

150 g/5½ oz French beans, tops trimmed

2 tbsp vegetable oil

1 garlic clove, finely chopped

6 spring onions, sliced

1 tsp chilli paste

2 tbsp soy sauce

2 tbsp rice wine

4 tbsp smooth peanut butter

3 tbsp coconut milk

METHOD

1 Cut the carrots diagonally into thin slices. Cut the cauliflower into small florets, then slice the stalk thinly. Thickly slice the pak choi. Cut the beans into 3-cm/1¼-inch lengths.

2 Heat the vegetable oil in a wok or large frying pan and stir-fry the garlic and spring onions for about 1 minute. Stir in the chilli paste and cook for a few seconds.

3 Add the carrots and cauliflower and stir-fry for 2–3 minutes.

4 Add the pak choi and beans and stir-fry for a further 2 minutes. Stir in the soy sauce and rice wine.

5 Mix the peanut butter with the coconut milk and stir into the pan, then cook, stirring, for a further minute. Serve hot.

FISH WITH COCONUT & BASIL

›Serves 4 ›Preparation time: 10–15 minutes ›Cooking time: 15 minutes

INGREDIENTS

2 tbsp vegetable oil

450 g/1 lb skinless cod fillet

25 g/1 oz seasoned flour

1 garlic clove, crushed

2 tbsp Thai red curry paste

1 tbsp fish sauce

300 ml/10 fl oz coconut milk

175 g/6 oz cherry tomatoes, halved

20 fresh basil leaves

fragrant rice, to serve

METHOD

1 Heat the vegetable oil in a preheated wok or large frying pan.

2 Using a sharp knife, cut the fish into large cubes, carefully removing any bones with a clean pair of tweezers.

3 Place the seasoned flour in a bowl. Add the cubes of fish and mix until well coated.

4 Add the coated fish to the wok and stir-fry over a high heat for 3–4 minutes, or until the fish just begins to brown at the edges.

5 In a small bowl, mix together the garlic, curry paste, fish sauce and coconut milk. Pour the mixture over the fish and bring to the boil.

6 Add the tomatoes to the mixture in the wok and leave to simmer for 5 minutes.

7 Roughly chop or tear the fresh basil leaves and add them to the wok. Stir carefully to combine, taking care not to break up the fish.

8 Transfer to serving plates and serve hot with fragrant rice.

RED PRAWN CURRY

> Serves 4 > Preparation time: 5–15 minutes > Cooking time: 15 minutes

INGREDIENTS

2 tbsp vegetable oil

1 garlic clove, finely chopped

200 ml/7 fl oz coconut milk

2 tbsp Thai fish sauce

1 tsp sugar

12 large raw prawns, deveined

2 lime leaves, finely shredded

1 small red chilli, deseeded and finely sliced

10 leaves Thai basil, if available, or ordinary basil

RED CURRY PASTE

3 dried long red chillies

$\frac{1}{2}$ tsp ground coriander

$\frac{1}{4}$ tsp ground cumin

$\frac{1}{2}$ tsp ground black pepper

2 garlic cloves, chopped

2 lemon grass stalks, chopped

1 kaffir lime leaf, finely chopped

1 tsp freshly grated root ginger or galangal, if available

1 tsp shrimp paste, optional

$\frac{1}{2}$ tsp salt

METHOD

1 To make the red curry paste, put all the ingredients in a blender and blend until smooth, adding a little water if necessary. Alternatively, pound the ingredients in a mortar and pestle. Set aside.

2 Heat the oil in a wok or large frying pan until almost smoking. Add the garlic and fry until golden. Add 1 tablespoon of the red curry paste and cook for a further minute. Add half the coconut milk, and the fish sauce and sugar. Stir well. The mixture should thicken slightly.

3 Add the prawns and simmer for 3–4 minutes until they begin to turn pink. Add the remaining coconut milk and the lime leaves and chilli. Cook for a further 2–3 minutes until the prawns are just tender.

4 Add the basil leaves, stir until wilted and serve hot.

GREEN CHICKEN CURRY

>Serves 4 >Preparation time: 5 minutes >Cooking time: 40–45 minutes

INGREDIENTS

6 boneless, skinless chicken thighs, cut into bite-sized pieces

400 ml/14 fl oz coconut milk

2 garlic cloves, crushed

2 tbsp Thai fish sauce

2 tbsp Thai green curry paste

12 baby aubergines, also called Thai pea aubergines

3 green chillies, finely chopped

3 kaffir lime leaves, shredded

4 tbsp chopped fresh coriander

boiled rice, to serve

METHOD

1 Pour the coconut milk into a wok or large frying pan. Bring to the boil over a high heat.

2 Add the chicken pieces, garlic and fish sauce to the wok and bring back to the boil. Lower the heat and simmer gently for about 30 minutes, or until the chicken is just tender.

3 Remove the chicken from the mixture with a perforated spoon. Set aside and keep warm.

4 Stir the green curry paste into the pan, add the aubergines, chillies and lime leaves and simmer for 5 minutes.

5 Return the chicken to the wok and bring to the boil. Adjust the seasoning to taste with salt and pepper, then stir in the coriander. Serve the curry with boiled rice.

LYCHEE & GINGER SORBET

>Serves 4   >Preparation time: 4½–5 hours

INGREDIENTS

2 x 400 g/14 oz cans lychees in syrup

finely grated rind of 1 lime

2 tbsp lime juice

3 tbsp stem ginger syrup

2 egg whites

TO DECORATE

starfruit slices

slivers of stem ginger

METHOD

1 Drain the lychees, reserving the syrup. Place the lychees in a blender or food processor with the lime rind, lime juice and stem ginger syrup and process until completely smooth. Transfer to a mixing bowl.

2 Mix the purée thoroughly with the reserved syrup, pour into a freezerproof container and freeze for 1–1½ hours until slushy in texture. (Alternatively, use an ice-cream maker.)

3 Remove the sorbet from the freezer and whisk to break up the ice crystals. Whisk the egg whites in a clean, dry bowl until stiff, then quickly and lightly fold them into the iced lychee mixture.

4 Return the sorbet to the freezer and freeze until firm. Serve the sorbet in scoops, decorated with starfruit and stem ginger.

MANGOES IN LEMON GRASS SYRUP

>Serves 4 >Preparation time: 1 hour >Cooking time: 5 minutes

INGREDIENTS

2 large, ripe mangoes

1 lime

1 lemon grass stalk, chopped

3 tbsp caster sugar

METHOD

1 Halve the mangoes, remove the stones and peel off the skins.

2 Slice the flesh into long, thin slices and gently arrange them in a wide serving dish.

3 Remove a few shreds of the rind from the lime and reserve for decoration, then cut the lime in half and squeeze out the juice.

4 Place the lime juice in a small pan with the lemon grass and sugar. Heat gently without boiling until the sugar has completely dissolved. Remove from the heat and allow to cool completely.

5 Strain the cooled syrup into a jug and pour evenly over the mango slices.

6 Scatter the mangoes with the reserved lime rind strips, cover and chill before serving.

INDEX